THE TOUCH

It took only a touch from my Saviour,
To know that He'd set me free,
Every wound and hurt He graciously healed –
A touch from my Saviour to me.

A touch from my Saviour renewed my mind,
A loving touch from the Lord,
A powerful touch of His Spirit,
Set me on fire, and ignited His Word.

A touch from the One who loves me,
And gave His life for mine,
Who built me up and remade me,
By the power of love divine.

How I love the touch of my Saviour!
I know I am never alone,
Oh, the love that caused my Saviour,
To touch me and make me His own.

MY HOPE AND STAR

In the silence of the night
And I feel you warm embrace,
I close my eyes and then, O Lord,
I see you, face to face.

I need you, oh so much, and yet
So far away you seem,
Caught up in worldly care and toil,
I can but dream and dream.

Love is so near, and yet so far,
I just stretch out and see,
How touching you, my Hope and Star,
Your love can flow through me.

*"I will bless the Lord who has
given me counsel. My heart also
instructs me in the night seasons."*
Psalm 16:7

SPIRIT FLIGHT

Sylvia Padilla

Haddenham
August, 2012

For Cassa,
with love in Jesus
& many
blessings!

Sylvia
(Macintosh)

HIS LOVE

Fearful heart be calm, be still,
I can all your longings fill,
Greater love you cannot find,
Than when you yield your heart and mind.

What else is there, but God's great love,
Flowing endless from above.
He holds you close and hears your sighs,
And wipes the tears from your eyes.

And fills the empty aching void,
That only He can fill,
And gives the happiness that comes,
From yielding to His will.

> *"Take my yoke upon you and
> learn from Me, for I am gentle
> and lowly in heart, and you will
> find rest for your souls."*
> *Matt. 11:29*

NEVER ALONE

Often I wonder as the days pass by,
Alone and sad, from my heart I cry – why?
Your plan, O Lord, is hard to follow,
When the way is fraught with pain and sorrow,
But Your arms hold me,
And Your love enfolds me.

Jesus, You're the lover of my soul,
You take up the pieces and make me whole,
You unloose the cords, my spirit freeing,
And Your love engulfs my being.

*"He has sent Me to heal the
broken-hearted, and proclaim
liberty to the captives." Isaiah 61:1*

HOLY FIRE

Let this earthen vessel shine
With the treasure I have within,
Holy Spirit, fire of God
Burnt out all my sin.

Clothed me in His wondrous flame,
Burnt away the dross,
Set my heart on fire for Him
When I met Him at the cross.

I'll not despise the sacrifice
My Saviour made for me,
In obedience I will walk
Because of His love for me.

O Holy Fire, burn on, burn on
And keep my heart afire,
And fill me with your boundless love –
Dear Lord, that's my desire.

*"We have this treasure in earthen
vessels, that the excellence of the
power may be of God and not of us."*
2 Cor. 4:7

MY COMFORTER

O Love! Lover of all Lovers,
Come secretly to me,
I need the warmth of your caresses,
And to share my love with Thee.

Only you and you alone
Can give me strength and life,
All others fail to fill my need,
You're my husband, I'm your wife.

Your love is all-encompassing,
You fill my yearning soul,
When I am lonely and in despair,
Your loving makes me whole.

Oh, how I need you, how I need you,
You're so above all earthly art,
You comfort me, and fill me so,
And mend my broken heart.

To you and only you I cling,
You, who were broken for me,
Your love is an eternal spring,
Bubbling, pure and free.

"Peace I leave with you, my peace I give you;
not as the world gives do I give to you. Let
not your heart be troubled, neither let it be
dismayed " John 14:27

BORN AGAIN

And now His love within me cries,
"You, yes, I love you!
The doors are opening, enter in
I will lead you through".

Wherefore did You come to me?
Beyond carnal touch I couldn't see,
A new life, a new world,
Before my expectant heart, unfurled.

Sensations coursing through my being,
I'm exposed to the All-Seeing,
Fear is washed in Love unbound,
My destiny at last is found.

Today is a new life beginning,
A joy in my Creator's loving,
Every day begins just so,
And I want the whole world to know.

Later on and deeper in
I began to see my sin.
Covered with shame I bent my head,
For I knew then why my Saviour bled.

He gently raised me from the ground.
And lifted me on high,
"For such as you, my dearest child,
I came on earth to die.

"It was my choice and even pleasure
To don an earthly frame,
To gather in my human treasure,
Each and every one by name.

"This moment is of joy complete,
And angels sing, "She's free!"
And now, my love, forever more,
You are part of me."

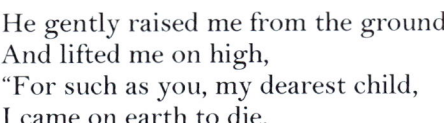

"If anyone is in Christ, he is a new creation;
old things have passed away; behold, all things
have become new." 2 Cor. 5:17

GOD'S GARDEN

God has planted his garden,
He's taken out the weeds,
He's filled my heart with flowers,
Destroyed the evil seeds.

Some weeds were deeply rooted,
It hurt to pull them out,
But oh, the joy that filled my garden
When freed from sin and doubt.

Let my heart be your garden, Lord,
Filled with flowers bright,
Perfumed, sweet and fresh as morning,
Dressed for your delight.

HEART CRY

Around the campfire burning, burning,
Flames are piercing the dark night's sky,
Gazing into the ardent fury
I find a reflection of my heart's cry.
A longing to consume with ardour
My short term upon this earth,
Not a day nor moment wasted,
May every second yield its worth.

*"I delight to do Your will, O my
God, and Your law is written
within my heart."*   **Psalm 40:8**

A DARK DAY'S TOUCH

A new page,
A new day,
Uncluttered,
A new way.

Yesterday is past,
It had me in its clutch
I couldn't escape its wrath –
A dark day's touch.

Negatives bombarded me,
I fought back!
I refused to be defeated,
I had let the angry wind attack.

It tried to batter me and shatter me,
I shook a little
But didn't stop,
I went straight on
Ignoring the onslaught.

Today, praise be to God
I made it through,
Yesterday is gone,
Today is new!

*"Thanks be to God, who
gives us the victory through
our Lord Jesus Christ." 1 Cor.15:57*

A SONG TO MY LORD

I shall sing a love song to my Lord,
His love is as the wind
That blows through the leaves
Of the yielding forest trees,
His caresses please.

O Lord, come closer, closer,
And hold me tight,
Whisper secrets in my ear,
Whispers in the night.

Smile like the moon on the plain,
Smile away my pain,
Hold me, oh hold me close,
Love of my life, I'll never lose.

Laugh like the streams
Rushing through my dreams,
Drops of liquid love,
Falling on my open heart,
Fill me to overflowing,
Closer to you growing,
Lord, my Love, my Life,
I am your sister, daughter, wife.

"For your Maker is your husband,
the Lord of Hosts is His Name."
                    Isaiah 54:5

LOVE OF GOD

What else is there but God's great love
Flowing endless from above.
He holds you close and hears your sighs
And wipes the tears from your eyes,
And fills the empty aching void
That only He can fill,
And gives the happiness that comes
From yielding to his will.

FIRST LOVE

Help me recapture the love
That was born in my soul long ago,
In times past I communed with You
In a way I now barely know.

In a moment of truth I feel once more,
As I used to love and live
And as divine love flows through me again,
I have so much more to give.

CHASTENED

Something happened today,
A revolution within my soul,
God's healing power descended
And made me, once again, whole.

I was bitter and resentful,
Yes, I was greatly oppressed,
I was looking down – so negative,
I forgot to remember I was blessed.

Abruptly my eyes were opened,
And I was shocked to see,
The direction in which I was headed,
With those I'd drag down with me.

I was shaken up, but faithful was He
To expose my sinful state of mind,
Now I'm trusting completely in Him,
Who is love, truth and mercy combined.

*"He also brought me out of a
horrible pit, out of the miry clay,
and set my feet upon a rock, and
established my steps." Psalm 40:2*

NEW BIRTH

Crying
Dying
Lying on my bed,
Mixed
Betwixt
Being alive and dead.
Part of me is living
Part of me is in pain,
Part of me is dying –
Oh, to be born again!"

Renewed!
Remade!
All in place.
I see His face!
Saved by His grace,
All torments now allayed.

*"For God so loved the world
that He gave His only begotten
Son, that whoever believes in
Him, should not perish but have
everlasting life." John 3:16*

REARRANGED

You change,
It's strange,
Life takes an unexpected turn,
You cast aside your treasured dreams,
Your plans come apart at the seams,
You find you're following unknown streams,
Your life is rearranged.

FANTASY LAND

To fantasize
Is pretty lies,
They entertain a while.
It amuses
And confuses,
Makes you laugh and cry and smile.
Your feet are off the ground
Your base for living unsound,
Alone in a world of dreams
Where nothing is quite as it seems
A world in which one tends,
To wonder why one has no friends.

MAGICAL MUSIC

Oh to fly on the wings of song
In the clear blue skies, that's where I belong,
And I leave the ground to the heavenly sound
Of melody, sweet and strong.

The earth and its cares fade swiftly away
As the magical notes relentlessly play,
And vibrate in my ears and bring forth tears
Of emotions, sensations, of love.
I pray.

Then bounding free and even higher
My heart thrills with unnamed desire,
As mysterious harmonies rise and fall
Engulfing my soul, my being, my all.

DECEIVED

I love to live in fantasy land
So come, I'll take you by the hand
And we can travel unknown skies
A blend of truth, coloured with lies.

A FEW THOUGHTS

I want to write to express myself
To share what God has done,
I want to show my fellow man
The wonder of His Son.

* * *

The Lord, the Holy One who lives
In the inmost part,
With His love and tenderness
Has conquered my cold heart.

* * *

Only He can take the burden,
Only He can calm the fears,
Only He unveils the secret
Of the reason for my tears.

* * *

Merciful Lord never gives up on us,
When we are faithless, disobedient and
dumb,
Plans A, B & C, He has lined up for us,
And never stops calling us, "Come!

* * *

Let me plant a seed of Love
Into the hardest heart,
And as that seed begins to shoot,
In two, that heart will part.

*"I will give you a new
heart, and put a new
spirit within you." Ez.36:26*

* * *

Daily I cry to the Saviour, my Friend
The One who has no beginning nor end,
Come Loving Spirit my heart to refill
To You I hand over this day and my will.

* * *

When the Spirit of God
Moves across my soul
And I'm borne onto the light,
Love suspending – never ending,
My spirit takes flight.

*"Whom have I in heaven
but You? And there is none
upon earth that I desire
beside You." Psalm 73:25*

AT DAYBREAK

I need this time alone with you,
To lean upon your breast,
To draw from your wellspring of love,
And put my heart to rest.

I need the quietness of the morn,
Under the shadow of your wing,
To raise my soul to heaven
And set my heart to sing.

I long to be alone with you,
To cleanse my heart and mind,
To give you all my cares and fears,
And know they're left behind.

Your Word is priceless treasure
I gather to my heart,
It gives me endless pleasure
And love and power to impart.

And in the stillness of the dawn,
I feel the fingers of your love
Encompass me and hold me fast,
Divine protection from above.

My time with you and with your Word
In the expectant dawn,
Is the highlight of my day,
For every day, love is reborn.

"When you said, 'seek my face',
my heart said unto you, 'Your
Face, Lord, I will seek.'" Psalm 27:8

ANSWERED PRAYER

As you wish it shall be done,
For he is my beloved son.
His life a sacrifice will be,
Because he truly pleases me.

I planned his life right from the start,
Each day has been a work of art,
Planned so, a vessel meet for use
A treasure I shall never lose.

HOPE

A thousand mines exploding in my head,
I wish that I were dead upon my bed.
But Jesus very quietly said,
"For your sins, I bled."

*"For as in Adam all die, even
so in Christ all shall be made
alive." 1 Cor:15:22*

TO HEAVEN AND BACK

"Come to the Sunny Isles
Of love and smiles –
Leap into the spirit."

"Will you show me how
To be in the Eternal Now?"

"Close your eyes,
Float above your bed,
A whirling, roaring sound
Courses through your head.

Dive in, Beloved,
Taste and see,
Float free,
Love me."

"Flying,
Dying?"

"Dear, I'm here forever,
Leave you? Never!

Descend from the Isle Bright
Back to earthly night.
Yet never alone,
For you have grown
Into a Star of Light."

SURRENDER

He has captivated me with His love
From starry skies beyond,
He fills my dreams
And all, it seems
That love, and only love
Can fill the yearning, hungry soul.
A vacuum,
A void,
Aching for fulfilment.
To be taken and utterly possessed
By the all-encompassing Love of God,
He who fills every little fault and fissure,
No dark corner left.
The light fills and transforms.
He makes the heart glow with new life,
New love,
Blessings running over to others,
Bless my soul, O Lord, and fill me anew!

*"This is the message which we have
heard from Him and declare to you,
that God is light and in Him is no darkness
at all." 1 John 1:5*

THE MOONBEAM DANCE

Come Little One, let's fly on a moonbeam,
Dance on a moonbeam
Sing on a moonbeam,
Come, Little One
Let's fly on a moonbeam
Until the day grows bright.

Hold my hand, I'll help you through,
You are only one,
With me, you are two.
Come, Little One,
Let's fly on a moonbeam
Until the day grows bright.

Come! Dance on a moonbeam, sing on a moonbeam
I, your Lover, am three,
Let's fly on a moonbeam,
Love on a moonbeam –
And the moonbeam, my love,
Is me!

Come, Little One, let's fly on a moonbeam,
Sing on a moonbeam,
Dance on a moonbeam,
Come, Little One,
Let's fly on a moonbeam,
Until the night takes flight!

SONG

Whither shall I go
Oh, whither shall I flee?
Follow, follow, follow me to eternity.

The wind it blows, I know not where,
Oh take me from this world of care.

Why do you tarry, why do you wait?
Come follow me, before it is too late.

Who can tell where the wind does blow?
But I know that I must go,
To follow, follow, follow Thee to eternity,
Oh follow, follow, follow me to eternity.

Jesus calls you, follow the throng
To love and peace, and joyous song.
He pipes His tune all day to thee,
Oh, follow, follow, follow Him – to Eternity.

MARTYR

A shot! No fear.
If you listen, you can hear
The silent musical vibrating
Of each atom rotating.

You just slide through
The spaces in between,
A little shimmer only
Will show where you have been.

Now you're in another dimension,
Left behind, the chaos and tension,
A new world opens to your vision,
Believe it! You're free from your prison.

Left behind in deathly silence
Earth, bound in Satanic alliance,
But you are free, birth-cord severed,
On earth they sigh, "Ah, he was martyred."

> *"When he opened the sixth seal, I saw*
> *the souls of those who had been slain*
> *for the Word of God and for the*
> *testimony which they held." Rev. 6:9*

THE SECOND COMING

Light fills the skies,
It dazzles the eyes,
They bow down and weep
At His Majesty's feet.
Their clothing is torn from their backs,
Naked before Him they fall,
And wretched and sinful
Prostrate before Him,
Wishing they'd heeded His call.

"*Then I saw heaven opened, and beheld
a white horse, and He who sat on him was
called Faithful and True, and in righteousness
He judges and makes war.*" *Rev.19:11*

CONFLICT

Conflict –
Do I or don't I?
Should I, or not?
Is it right, is it wrong,
Have I lost the plot?
Is what I want the best for me?
And do I really need it?
His Word is clear, I must confess
And so I'd better heed it!

MONSOON

Where is the rain, why do we thirst?
Why do we wither and die?
The ground is parched,
Cracked and brown – why?

We droop so sadly, the birds chirp madly
Calling for the rain,
What did we do for you to desert us?
Don't you know, you really hurt us?
When will you visit again?

Every day now clouds have gathered,
Lifting our hearts' hopes high,
But the wind comes and blows them away,
Dear God, another thirsty day, we cry.

Today the clouds are gathered lower,
The heat's intense, all life moves slower,
The sun beats fiercely on the ground,
All is still, there is no sound.

Crack! A jagged streak on high
In a fractured moment illuminates the sky!
A sonorous rumble fills the air,
And the wind blows wildly the crazed trees'
hair.

Splash! One large drop,
Then two, now twenty,
The storm clouds freely give of their plenty.
All living creatures flee for cover,
Praise be to God! The drought is over!

GOD'S ART WORK

Things lovely and beautiful
The world despises,
Yet oft within the chaos,
A pure soul arises
Amongst the weeds, a flower,
Glorious in its grimy bower.
How long will such beauty survive?
Breath of God will keep it alive.
How is it that one could be
So alone and yet so lovely?
Beauty is hid in the faceless morass
Of humanity, loud, stupid, crass.
Who can recognise a work of art,
A vision perfected by God's own heart?
Yet love's sweet breath can bring to birth
A tender bloom from barren earth.

*"Like a lily among thorns, so is my
love among the daughters."*
Song of Songs 2:2

LOVE'S CREATION

I made the sparrows,
I made the trees,
I made creation
The way that I please.

It's all a reflection
Of my great love,
A manifestation
Of power from above.

And though you can't see
The way that it's done,
The mysterious wisdom
Of Father, Spirit and Son,

The marvels of nature
Speak plainly to all
Of My great design
For all, great and small.

"For since the creation of the world His invisible attributes are clearly seen, being understood by the things that are made." **Romans 1:20**

ON BEING THANKFUL FOR THE LITTLE THINGS IN LIFE

Thank you Lord, for the little things,
The simple joys that living brings,
Tiny bird with outstretched wings,
Alights on bough and sweetly sings.

Thank you Lord, for the little pleasures,
Stored in my heart like priceless treasures,
Such love shown me is without measure
That I can dwell upon at leisure.

Thank you for the refreshing breeze
That whispers softly through the trees,
She murmurs, "I just want to please,
And set you heart and mind at ease."

Thank you Lord, for a little pause
In the day's routine of chores,
One moment with You – my spirit soars,
And peace of mind once more restores.

*"In everything give thanks, for
this is the will of God in Christ
Jesus concerning you." 1 Thess. 5:18*

GOD'S CREATION

Cool wind, sunlit trees,
Rustling leaves, my senses please.

Early morning, new day dawning,
My soul calming to nature's loving.

Precious seeds fall to the earth,
Nature's womb, to give fresh birth,

Nurtured by the cool sweet rain,
In replica to live again.

A squirrel leaps from bough to bough
With a precision I know not how.

His flight takes me on a fantasy,
To a world where I can never be.

Refreshing rain, sunlight, dew,
Cool winds, all nature my soul renew.

> *"The Lord by wisdom founded the earth, by understanding He established the heavens; by His knowledge the depths were broken up, and clouds drop down the dew."* **Proverbs 3:19 & 20**

EVENING

Fluffy clumps of cloud
Reflect the end of day,
A burst of colours, red, blue, gold,
The sun casts his dying ray.

Silhouettes against the sky,
Swoop back and forth,
Winged mystery,
Calling, plaintive, cry.

Lady Moon arises,
Silver queen of night,
Transparent pale, against the blue,
She puts the day to flight.

Now in full majesty she sheds
Her bright reflected gleam,
And through the starry black expanse
Her shafts of silver stream.

"When I consider Your heavens,
the work of Your fingers, the moon
and the stars which You have ordained,
what is man that You are mindful of him,
and the son of man that You visit him?"
Psalm 8:3 & 4

36

IN PRAISE OF TREES

I wish I could paint a picture in leaves,
On a canvas of forest trees.
Redwoods, birches, oaks and elms,
Colours borrowed from other realms.
In three dimensions all would be,
To show my praises to a tree.

BAY BRIDGE

Fiery lights blazing a trail across the Bay,
San Francisco at the end of day.
Hurried workers rushing home,
Chasing before the evening's gloam.
Jewelled columns, standing bright,
Glowing sentinels of the night,
Pierce the sky with artificial flame,
Putting the evening stars to shame.

CHRISTMAS IN COSTA RICA

The spirit of Christmas has changed this year,
It is not the same as before, I fear.
The excitement and fun of years gone by
Is missing this year – I wonder why?

There's noise in the streets, cacophonous sounds,
Strident horns, the people like clowns,
Vendors selling their wares in the streets,
Imported apples, plastic toys and oversized sweets.

Shoppers milling all about me,
Confusion rushing all around me,
Endless queues for the buses await me,
And alas! The money makers have found me.

Other Christmases I've known
Have gone, vanished – they have flown.
It seems a shame that it's not the same,
But the reason being, I have to own,
Is that this year, my dear, I've grown!

"Do not love the world or the things in
the world. If anyone loves the world, the
love of the Father is not in him. For all
that is in the world, the lust of the flesh,
the lust of the eyes and the pride of life,
is not of the Father, but of the world."
1 John 2:15 & 16

A MOTHER'S ROLE

Only you can know, the yearning in my breast
To do my all for you and give my very best.
I fail so often, fall so short, I feel so useless and so small,
Please use this weak tool of yours, my everything, my all.

I doubt within my mind, about my daily tasks,
Is this my job, my role in life, or is there more He asks.
I know I could do better and be more faithful to His Word,
The times I'm truly happy are when I'm yielded to my Lord.

I should be happy just to love Him,
But why do I feel the way I do?
It's an uphill struggle all the way, (why is it so hard to pray?)
I cannot seem to get away to do the things I need to.

The children call and bother, I need to help them more,
Oh why, when it is my desire, burning in me like a fire,
It seems so oft to be a chore,
Just like any other?

The flesh, that is the reason, it holds me back and
                                                    dominates,
And bears upon my willing spirit, like so many
                                                    hundredweights.
Help me Lord, to be faithful, for that is what I truly need,
To put each idea and plan, into action and in deed.

Plan and organise my day,
Take time for love and work and play,
Be an example, good and strong,
Encourage right and chastise wrong.

I need wisdom and strength Lord,
Constancy and love,
Obedience to your Word, Lord,
And power from above!

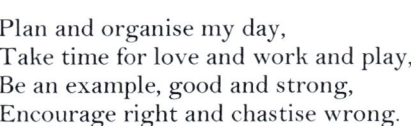

"...let us lay aside every weight, and the sin which so easily ensnares us, and let us run with endurance the race that is set before us, looking unto Jesus, the Author and Finisher of our faith." Hebrews 12:1

ADOLESCENCE

Aspirations, hopes and fears,
Laughter, anxiety, foolishness, tears,
Dreams beyond possibility,
A night-time life of fantasy.

Adolescence' cup is full,
Disillusion – life is cruel,
Mother, father, not the same,
Brothers, sisters – all to blame.

No-one can do anything right,
Especially you, young gallant knight,
Who faces dragons to gain fair maiden,
Then Dad calls out, "Clear up the garden"!

And you, sweet pretty budding flower,
Ensconced in your fairy bower,
Fashion, romance, dreamy wishes,
Mum calls out, "Clear up the dishes!"

SISTERS

Big girl and little girl
Together quietly walk,
Big girl and little girl,
I love to hear them talk.

Big girl graciously inclined,
Little one with upturned face,
Big sister listens, gentle kind,
Hands big and small enlaced.

UNDER THE MANGO TREE

Ten Years and Two Years
Together closely sat today
Under the sunshade hand in hand,
Watching brothers play.

Ten Years has striped kitty
Cosy on her knee,
Two Years sitting next to ten years
Under the mango tree.

Eight Years and Seven Years
After the ball they run,
With Ten and Two years watching,
The game is much more fun!

THROUGH THE DOOR

My Darling has passed through the Door.
It's hard to realise I'll see her no more,
A tree she grew –
To wither, oh too soon,
From birth to death
A life, always in bloom.
And this frail tree bore fruit untold,
Too lovely to mar, by growing old.

And when I saw my darling child
In Jesus' arms –
I smiled.

*My beloved spoke and said
to me, 'Rise up my love, my
fair one, and come away.'"*
Song of Songs 2:10

AT HIS WORD

Earth is but a bubble in time,
Suspended by the breath of God,
Marvellous are Your works, O Lord,
Brought into being by Your Word.

Beyond is the eternal now,
Fashioned by Your hand,
Where words take shape,
And thoughts are real,
And mysteries shall be revealed,
In that Heavenly Land.

"By the Word of the Lord the heavens were made, and all the host of them by the breath of God." Proverbs 33:6

ESCAPE

I met a man,
A lonely man
Whose heart was searching deep,
He thought he had a kind of solution,
And kept himself in perpetual motion
So as not to think and weep.

STILL SEARCHING

You have captured my heart and my
mind,
Yet my spirit remains free,
We are one of a kind
You and me.
A look, a smile, encouragement,
Something not said – just sent,
Can I guess how you feel?
You'll never tell,
Because even you don't know very
well.

Conflicting emotion
Like waves of the ocean
Ebbing and flowing,
Waning and growing,
Not really knowing
How to be free – like me!

A LOVE LETTER

Dearest Love,
I love you,
I want you,
I behold you
And close myself about you.
I would become one with you,
Knowing you innermost thoughts,
And feelings,
And longings.
Become one beside you,
Within you
Round about you.

I would help you,
I would feed you
And give you my all.
Will you take me?
Embrace me?
Shall we grow strong?
Wonderful Love – to you I belong.

LOST, THEN FOUND

O Wandering Star,
Treading the Universe,
Looking for your lost orbit.
Will you ever find it?
The years drag by,
Oh, weariness!
Enlightened now and then by chance encounter
With another celestial body,
Or touching momentarily one in his own orbit,
And then rejected,
And thrown even further out, and out,
Lost in darkness,
Lost in space,
Until you find the Everlasting Arms
Who will hold you and embrace you
And gently place you in your own orbit,
Where you will shine brightly and gloriously forever
A joy to beholders,
And all the stars will rejoice and sing
The eternal love song of God.

THE END OF THE SEARCH

How I wish that you were here,
Enigmatic soul!
With the yearning deep within your breast
To be whole.

Always searching, looking for the truth,
I gave it you,
Now you're gone – alone again,
I still love you.

You found Jesus, did you know it?
Do you realise
You search is over? I could see it
In your eyes.

When you walk amongst the hills,
Praise Him.
When you are alone with your thoughts,
Hear Him.

No matter how they treat you,
You're not alone,
No matter how fate will meet you,
You'll come home.

> *"And this is the testimony: that*
> *God has given us Eternal Life,*
> *and that life is in His Son."*
> *John 5:11*

DO YOU REALLY LOVE ME?

Why do you read about Me,
Talk about Me,
Even shout about Me?
Why do you praise Me to others,
Boasting of your espousal to Me
With you sisters and brothers?

How can you say you love Me,
If you never talk with Me,
Laugh with Me,
Nor cry with Me,
Or even say, "Hi" to Me?

Don't you know I love you?
Yearn for you
Burn for you.
Long to hear you utter,
"I love You."

I want you to say:
"I can't live without You,
I shall never doubt You.
You are my very life,
I am your adoring wife,
And I love everything about You."

*"And I have declared to them
You Name, and will declare it;
that the love with which You have
loved Me may be in them, and I in
them." John 17:26*

MY GOALS

You ask me, "What are your goals?"
To live each day as if it were the last,
A little thought for the future,
Forget the past!

To find a soul who needs some love
And try to fill that lack,
To show another way to live,
Off the beaten track.

The beaten track is for beaten men,
Whose lives are programmed so,
But my horizon soars beyond,
Yet alone I will not go.

So come with me and take my hand
I'll show you true love's door,
That leads into eternity
Where death shall be no more.

*"By this we know love because
he laid down His life for us, and
we also ought to lay down our
lives for the brethren." 1 John 3:16*

PLAN ZEE

I failed again!
How many times more
Must I pick myself
Up from the floor?
I've missed Plan A, as well as B,
I also flunked Plans C & D,
A hopeless case I must be,
'Cause I chickened out of F & E.

I tried so hard,
To no avail,
The plans came back
In red, marked "Fail!"
So many plans
Back on the shelf,
Messed up by me,
My worldly self!

Then a light bulb switched
Inside my head,
"Not my way,
But the Lord's, instead"!
It's not too late
To do his will,
While I have breath
He'll use me still.

He never gave up on me, you see,
For all the time He had plan Zee!

WHILST TRYING TO WRITE A REPORT

I feel like sitting and dreaming,
Not writing a chronicled account,
My thoughts fly hither and thither,
To much, they do not amount.

I love to play with my thoughts,
As they run the range of the rainbow,
Who can tell where they may end?
O where my spirit may go?

Elusive as they may be,
And much they do not achieve,
They please and entertain me,
By the intricate pattern they weave.

Inside out and round about,
Round about and inside out,
Back to front and upside down,
From head to toe, and toe to crown.

Now it's time to return to earth
And put my thoughts in ship-shape form,
Down I come, I pick up my pen,
Dear chronicle – I'm back to norm.

DREAMING

Simple things appeal to me,
Sitting with you, drinking tea,
With both our minds on a distant star,
Sitting knee to knee.

You meet my gaze and utter a phrase
Delightful to my ear,
I look at you, a little shy
At the gentle words I hear.

You have a depth you don't realise,
I can tell as I look in your loving eyes,
And I wish to be longer each time with you,
To discover, more deeply you heart, kind and true.

Time's up – we must part
Until next time, dear heart,
I will be waiting, ready with tea
Dreams from afar, with you next to me.

VICE VERSA

If I were you and you were me,
Just think how happy we would be.
I'd know your thoughts and needs so well,
If in your body my spirit should dwell.

And you would know just how I feel,
What is false and what is real.
I couldn't hide a single thought –
(If I thought something I shouldn't,
I'd soon get caught!)

So although the advantages are great, I'm sure,
And I'd like to try it one day,
We could get quite confused,
And somewhat bemused,
So I prefer in my body to stay.

OPEN THE DOOR

Let the light shine through the darkness,
Let the light shine through the pain,
Let the whole world know that my Lover,
Gave me power to be born again.

He sought me and He found me,
In this dark world's strife,
He found me and He loved me,
And filled my empty life.

This love and light is for everyone,
Not a gift only for me,
I want to share this wonderful love
With everyone I see.

There's no need to cry in the darkness
With no guide to show the way.
You only have to open the door
And the night will turn to day.

*"Behold, I stand at the door and
knock. If anyone hears my voice and
opens the door, I will come in to him and
dine with Him and he with me." Rev. 3:20*

PROPHECY

Take, eat of my body to set you free,
I am He who died on the tree,
You need faith to believe what you can hear,
So listen now and lend your ear.

My love's unending, tender and sweet,
Remember I washed my disciples' feet.
Humble yourself and become a man,
And humble yourself to follow My plan.
Where will you go, and what will you see?
Just come to me on bended knee,
And I will show you wonders untold,
Of stories new and stories old.

I will show you the way, do not fear,
For you are mine and are very dear.
Hold on my love, hold on to me tight,
And I will lead you through this dark night.
I am the Light to guide your way,
Come my love, come and stay
Close by my side, and you'll ever be
Wrapped in my love, and dearest to me.

"Where shall I go, and what shall I find?"
You can't work it out in your carnal mind.
Let go and let God have His wonderful way,
And true peace of mind will have come to stay.
Praise Your Name, O Lord of Light.
I love you my Saviour.,
Be near him tonight.

GOD'S MERCY

My soul within me cries,
"Release!"
My soul within me cries,
"Will this pain ever cease?"

A prisoner in chains, I am
Fettered by the bonds of flesh,
I want out – now!" I cry,
My tangled thoughts enmeshed.

It comes, it goes, it sinks, it flows,
The light – the darkness deep,
I thought by taking my own way out
I'd find eternal sleep.

And now I'm spinning round and
round,
There is no sky, there is no ground,
I'm all alone, and no-one knows
That I am here – nothing shows.

I call in vain, they cannot hear
This torment I can hardly bear,
I need that someone show me where
Reality can be found.

A hand appears—a light behind,
A guide has come to ease my mind.
Thank God! I am alone no more,
Wait! Yes! – I see the other shore.

THE WORD

There're no words to express how I feel,
When I realise your word is real.
It thrills me and fills me and makes me believe,
With you coming through
I can everything lovely, achieve.

Oh, the boundless grace and the wonderful truth
That is shed in my heart by your word.
You are holy and beautiful, wonderful Lord,
And my love has no way to express
My gratitude for the magnitude
Of you sacrifice for my sinfulness.

I love you and give you my heart,
My body, my life and my soul.
They are yours, dear Lord, to do as you please,
Oh thank you, for making me whole.

SPIRIT ETERNAL

At my heart's beating, youth is fleeting,
Beauty is but for a season,
But the spirit still controls my will,
My heart and mind and reason.

Though all may yield to time's decay,
And corruption takes its hold,
My spirit, fed by Love Eternal
Never will grow old.

It's often held that beauty
Is life's crowning glory,
Yet the inner light that shines within
Tells another story.

So when my mirror reflects the years,
I've passed in earthly realm,
I thank God for the years I've spent
With Jesus at my helm.

*"For now we see in a mirror, dimly,
but then face to face, now I know in
part, but then I shall know just as I
am known."*   Cor. 13:12

SPIRIT FLIGHT

I had to get it out!
I couldn't keep it in,
My soul was yearning, craving,
longing,
Something exploded within!

How could I express it?
The need to cry, to shout, to sing.
Then heaven opened up its gates,
And my spirit took wing!

I soared above the earthly plane,
I revelled in its glorious light,
Free! Free! I cried, how wonderful,
Earthbound body – spirit flight!

YOUR ROLE

Do you believe in destiny
In this world's chaotic dance?
Were you sent, or did you choose
The role you're playing (win or lose)
Or is it all by chance?

Are you guided day by day, by an unseen
hand?
Or do you, like an unmanned train
Rush headlong through life's joy and pain
To an unknown land.

If you are tempted every so often
To feel you could have bettered your part,
Remember life is but a schooling
To the end right from the start.

Success is in the eyes of man,
God sees it in a different way,
So do you thank Him for what you've got
Or do you complain about your lot?
Do you bother to pray?

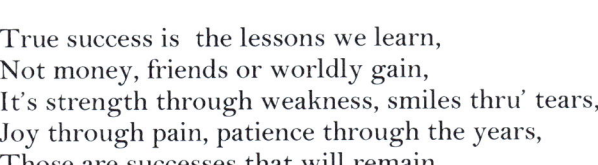

True success is the lessons we learn,
Not money, friends or worldly gain,
It's strength through weakness, smiles thru' tears,
Joy through pain, patience through the years,
Those are successes that will remain.

And what is the greatest lesson to learn?
Surely it has to be love,
To love the unlovely, to suffer the bore,
To lift up the weak and be kind to the poor,
These are the lessons in life from above.

*"And do not present your members as
instruments of unrighteousness to sin
but present yourselves to God as being
alive from the dead, and your members
as instruments of righteousness to God."*
Romans 6:13

Notes to some of the poems

5 - THE TOUCH
Joy at being set free from spiritual bondage.

11 - BORN AGAIN
This was inspired by Karine, a young Belgian girl who found the Lord in Costa Rica.

13 - GOD'S GARDEN
Gratitude for being set free.

15 - A SONG TO MY LORD
This poem came line by line as I was listening to a Russian folk song.

17 - CHASTENED
I wrote this after a truly horrible and fearful dream showed me how harbouring evil towards someone was grieving the Holy Spirit and damaging to me and others.

23 - AT DAYBREAK
In India I used to get up early and take time on my own on the roof away from everybody.

27 - THE MOONBEAM DANCE
Life was difficult for me and my children when we were living in Mexico so I took this little flight of fantasy.

32 - GOD'S ART WORK
I was sitting on a crowded and fetid bus in San Jose, Costa Rica, and wrote this as it bumped its way through the dirty, narrow streets.

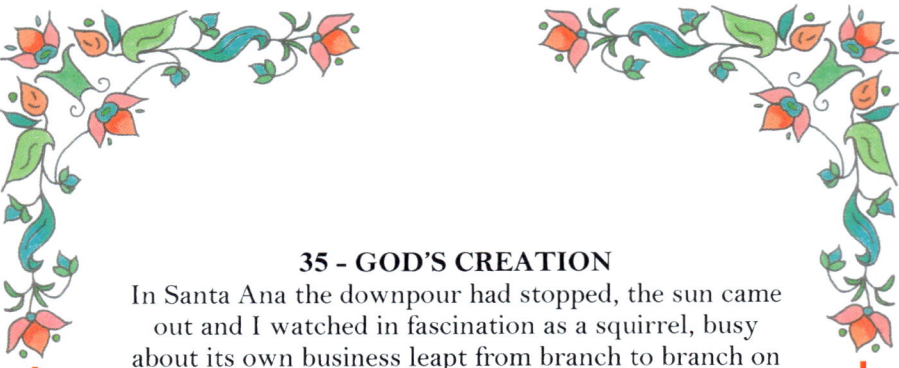

35 - GOD'S CREATION
In Santa Ana the downpour had stopped, the sun came out and I watched in fascination as a squirrel, busy about its own business leapt from branch to branch on the tree outside my window.

36 - EVENING
Another snatched moment in India on the roof at dusk.

37 - IN PRAISE OF TREES, BAY BRIDGE
Autumn in Berkley, California

42 - SISTERS
Victoria and Cristiana in the garden in Santa Ana

42 - UNDER THE MANGO TREE
Victoria and Cristiana watching Emanuel and David play football.

43 - THROUGH THE DOOR
Claudia (Shuly), who left us for a better world shortly before her eighteenth birthday.

44 - ESCAPE
This was a businessman I met whose wife had recently died.

48 - THE END OF THE SEARCH
This is about one of the many foreign visitors to Costa Rica who found the Lord.

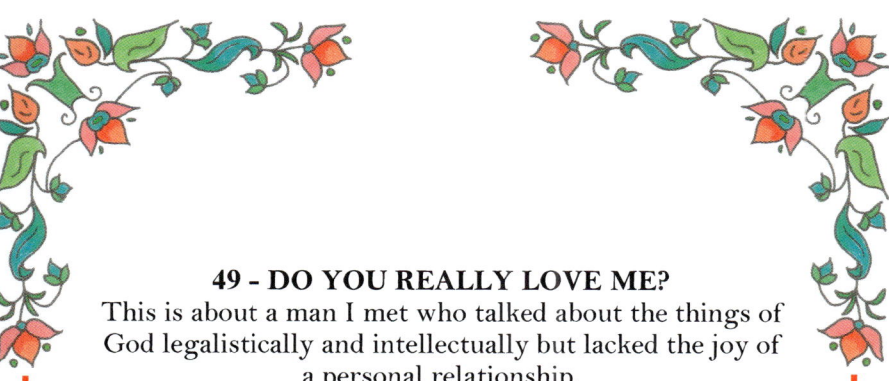

49 - DO YOU REALLY LOVE ME?
This is about a man I met who talked about the things of God legalistically and intellectually but lacked the joy of a personal relationship.

56 - PROPHECY FOR A CHILD OF GOD
Someone I knew well was having a very hard time. I woke up in the night and jotted this down, not realising it was a poem until I read it in the morning.

57 - GOD'S MERCY
A terminally ill man I met in Costa Rica, in desperation took his own life.

58 - THE WORD
Joy in the healing power of the Scriptures.

59 - SPIRIT ETERNAL
One morning in my late forties I noticed a few wrinkles and got this little inspiration.

Printed in Great Britain
by Amazon

71439268R00037